TO THE
WORLD'S GREATEST
~~FATHER~~
FARTER

Published by Sellers Publishing, Inc.
Copyright © 2020 Sellers Publishing, Inc.
Illustrations © 2020 Donna Stackhouse
All rights reserved.

Sellers Publishing, Inc.
161 John Roberts Road, South Portland, Maine 04106
Visit our website: www.sellerspublishing.com • E-mail: rsp@rsvp.com

Charlotte Cromwell, Production Editor

ISBN 13: 978-1-5319-1209-3

10 9 8 7 6 5 4 3 2 1

Printed in China.

TO THE
WORLD'S GREATEST
~~FATHER~~
FARTER

by Toots Amore
Illustrated by
Donna Stackhouse

SELLERS
PUBLISHING

You always say
"the dog's to blame."
But we know that
excuse is lame.

The puppy howls,
the flowers droop

It sticks to all the walls like paint.
A whiff or two will make you faint.

We open all the
windows wide.
We gasp for air,
then run outside!

And later on,
inside our tent,
we woke up to
an awful scent.

Your farts could kill,
Dad, there's no doubt.
But that's not all
this book's about.

So on this very special
day we want to take
the time to say . . .

You make life happy,
safe, and fun.

Because
we REALLY
love you,
Dad